Clarissa's Crossing

THE
LATTER-DAY DAUGHTERS
SERIES

No portion of this book may be reproduced in any form without
written permission from the publisher, Aspen Books, 6211 S. 380 W,
Salt Lake City, UT 84107

Library of Congress Cataloging-in-Publication Data
Clarissa's Crossing by Launi K. Anderson.
p.cm. – (Latter-day Daughters series : 2)
Summary: Clarissa sneaks her kitten on board when she and her family
travel from England to America as converts to the Mormon Church in the
mid-1800s.
ISBN - 1-56236-500-2
[1. Mormons–fiction. 2. Voyages and travels–fiction.
3. Cats–Fiction.] I. Title. II. Series.
PZ7.A54375C1 1995
[Fic]–dc20   95-16734
                                                    CIP

10 9 8 7 6 5 4 3 2

CLARISSA'S CROSSING

THE
LATTER-DAY DAUGHTERS
SERIES

Launi K. Anderson

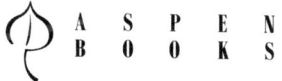

ASPEN
BOOKS

Dedication

To the Latter-day Daughters in my life:
April, Lyndi, Jillian, Laurie, Mom and Nanny.
And to Devon, with love.

Acknowledgments

I wish to thank my family for the love and support
it takes to pull stories out of the sky.
Also to Adrienne,
for dreaming of the little girls who color Church history and
whose legacy we now share.

TABLE OF CONTENTS

Chapter 1
Saying Good-bye 1

Chapter 2
Spies Among Us 9

Chapter 3
A Secret Shared .14

Chapter 4
Topside 20

Chapter 5
Good Advice 27

Chapter 6
The Brew 34

Chapter 7
Father's Fur Coat 40

Chapter 8
"Lost" at Sea 47

Chapter 9
The Fever 54

Chapter 10
New Eyes 61

Glossary 69
What Really Happened 72

'Tis with joy I am bidding farewell,
To the proud boasted land of my birth,
I go with the upright to dwell,
Where the pure will find heaven on earth.
It is faith, 'tis not fancy that paints,
The vision of bliss that I see,
I go to the home of the Saints,
To Zion, the land of the free.

excerpt from
"Farewell to the Land of My Birth"
by Ann Cash
(*Millennial Star*, April 14, 1855)

CHAPTER ONE

Saying Good-Bye

"Ah, look at her, Miles," Father said to our coachman. "Am I not a lucky man to have such a flower in my garden?"

"Aye, sir," Miles said, "that you are."

I tried coming down the stairs as though I hadn't heard them, but I couldn't cheat Father out of seeing me blush. With my gray traveling cloak draped loosely around my shoulders, I took each step in a slow, ladylike fashion. Mrs. Goodwin of the Manchester Ladies School would have been proud.

"See how we wait on her then?" Father nudged Miles and winked.

"And a pleasure it is, to be sure." Miles looked up the stairway at me and nodded. "Morning Miss," he said, then hurried out the door with my small black trunk.

"Come now, love," Father said. "Our little Andrew is already in the carriage and waiting. We'd best join him quickly. Don't we know, he'd have no fear of driving the horses to Liverpool himself and leaving us behind."

I took his hand and stepped back. "Father, wait," I said. "Tell me one more time how it will go. I do wish to be the good, sweet girl you want, but I'm full of knots inside." Father sat back on the stairs and pulled me next to him. Miles came in again and hoisted the last trunk onto his back, then hurried out, pulling the door shut with his foot.

"Clarissa," Father said, "you mustn't be afraid. We'll be taking the carriage to the ports at Liverpool. There, we will board the packet ship* Wilmott. She's a shining new beauty. President Henderson will meet us on board, along with much of our branch—sixty-three of them to be precise."

"But how?" I said. "How have they managed it? Most of them have so little money to spare."

"We've waited and prayed for this day, dear. And now the Lord has opened up the way. Our own promised land awaits us."

Father always got a dreamy, far-off look on his

face when he talked about leaving England, almost as if he were seeing something that took his breath away.

"I've known," he said, "since the first day I heard Brother Spencer preach in town, that his message was an answer to my prayers. He told us that through the blessings of the temple we could be sealed together as a family. We needn't worry that we'll never see your dear mother again, Lord rest her soul." He brushed his fingers against my cheek. "If a temple is to be built in Zion, we must go there. Clarissa, this is our dream!"

My mother. Though I was only seven when she died, Father had kept her alive to Andrew and me with stories of her laughter, goodness, and grace. He saw to it that she was more to us than the beautiful, dark-eyed woman in the oak-framed portrait.

"But America, Father," I sighed, "it's so far away. What do we know of it? Aunt Polly's letters sound so grand, but I've heard many other stories. And what of our home, our things," here my voice caught, "and Lillibeth?" I tried not to let my chin tremble. Father was so excited and I hadn't the heart to spoil it for him.

From the moment he was baptized every patient in Father's care had to hear about the Book of

Mormon. Father would say this gospel felt like a fire burning inside him. Over the years, dozens of our friends and family were converted by his teaching as the fire touched them as well.

"I know," he said, "it is not an easy thing to walk away from one life and step into another without glancing back a bit. But our house and home* will be well taken care of by the Johnstons. They could never hope to buy a place like this, not in a hundred years. And with all their wee ones, they'll be so happy to have a nook of their own. And we are glad to give it, aren't we?"

Father was so generous and kind. He truly thought nothing of parting with all that we knew. Our whole world would be drifting away from us, and he didn't seem a bit worried. But it was not as easy for me to leave behind all our lovely things, though I couldn't say so.

"And about Lillibeth," he went on, "there just aren't many people who will offer to care for a kitten."

"But, Father," I said quietly, "I've never liked Mrs. Turpin. She scowls at us so. And I've heard . . ."

"Now, Clarissa," he said, "you mustn't believe schoolyard tales."

4

"But they're not just tales, Father. She told me herself that we oughtn't to have listened to 'those poisonous Mormons.' She says we are plain fools to follow that Joe Smith and his gold bible."* I gazed down at the floor. "She even says you've lost any sense you had, selling our things and giving away our home to make this trip."

"Well," Father laughed, "perhaps I have, but we're doing the right thing and I know we'll manage fine. Mrs. Turpin should be pleased to have a sweet kitty like your Lillibeth. I would wager she is in the old girl's lap this very moment. Now, let's have a smile."

I looked around at our beautiful home. The laces and shawls* made by my own mother. The frames and chairs and the rosebud tea set with the silver trim. Why must we leave it all? I still wondered, although Father had explained a dozen times that there was a long, hard journey ahead of us, and we would only have room to take a few of our belongings. "Enjoy the people," Father would say. "They are more important than things."

I leaned into his shoulder and sighed, "I *am* trying to be brave."

"And you're doing a fine job," he said. "Buck up now or Andrew will see your red eyes and worry for you. Allow this to be his great adventure and he will be better off for it."

"Go out to him then, Father," I said. "I'll be along. I intend to look about one last time, say my good-byes, and then be done with it."

"There's my good girl!" he said. "Hop it* now or the packet shall leave us and we'll be left swimming to America." Father winked again, as he often did to make me smile.

"I'll hurry," I promised. He arose, kissed my forehead, and closed the door behind him. There I was, left alone in our big, warm house to wander about one last time.

Walking past the large mirror by the drawing room I tried hopelessly to smooth down my unruly red curls. I pulled at my eyes so they wouldn't look so puffy, then patted my cheeks, hoping the color in my face would even out.

I walked back through the kitchen and across the creaky wooden floor. At first it made the usual faint squeaking noise, but with each step it sounded more and more like a baby wailing. Standing very still, I realized that my feet were not making the pitiful sound at all. Straining to hear from what direction it was coming, I held my breath. It seemed to be somewhere outside the back porch.

Unlatching the door was frightening, as the crying sound became more frantic. Trying to be cautious, I opened it just a small crack, but flung the door wide at what I saw. There on the step was a limp ball of matted fur. To my horror I realized it was my Lillibeth—though no one would have recognized her as she was.

Sitting in a wet heap with mud clotted and caked on her small body, Lillibeth was no longer the dainty fluff she'd been. Now she was merely a tiny, drenched and quivering thing with her head tipped to one side. It was as though she'd used all her strength to drag herself up into the yard.

"What has happened to you?" I shrieked. Scooping her up onto my arm, I noticed a small string tied around her neck with a loop dangling at one end. I'd once heard boys bragging in the schoolyard about tying a rock around a kitten's neck and daring one another to toss it into the pond. "My poor darling. Someone has tried to drown you!" I sobbed.

Running back through the kitchen I found the bread knife and carefully cut the string that was nearly choking my kitten. With the noose gone, she could breathe easier and the hoarse wailing stopped. With the last cupful of water left in the scrubbing bucket I rinsed off the mud as best I could. Searching through the rag bin I found a good-sized piece of flannel and wrapped her gently in it.

"That wicked woman," I said aloud, petting the half-dead body. "How could she be so cruel to a tiny helpless animal? And after giving Father her word that she would keep you safe."

I was too angry to think right. But what should I do? There was no time for careful planning. Father and Andrew were waiting outside, and one of them was sure to come fetch me at any moment.

"Don't you worry," I said, picking up my small carpetbag and setting my jaw firmly. "You're safe with me, and I won't let you go again." With that, I opened the bag and tenderly laid her inside with the few precious things I was allowed to bring.

"Clarissa, come along!" came Father's voice from the carriage. I glanced around the room one more time, snatched a simple linen handkerchief from the mantlepiece, and flew out the door.

"I'm ready, Father," I called. "We can go now!"

CHAPTER TWO

Spies Among Us

"I'm quite certain, miss," chuckled a voice behind me, "that we can find you something more suitable to eat than garbage." At first I froze, one hand still in the dreadful scrap bucket; then with a great sigh I stood up and slowly turned around.

Standing behind me was that same fellow I'd seen while boarding the ship, days ago. I assumed he was a member of the crew. He had offered to help with my things that day but I had refused. I could not trust anyone with my carpetbag. Not even Father. Not yet.

"Perhaps," he said, "I might bring your family more crackers or rice. That is, if you're this hungry." He looked as though he might laugh right out loud. It made me furious. Bad enough to be spotted in this hot, steaming galley,* but now to be teased about it was unbearable.

Lillibeth could not eat the hard dried fish and jerky we'd been given with our first week's provisions when we came aboard. She was too weak to chew it. So far, she'd only taken water out of my hand, then gone back to sleep. My only hope for her now was to find her something softer to eat.

"So?" the boy asked, bracing his arm against the doorway. He knew he was blocking my only means of escape.

"So, what?" I said, pretending to be calm. Never in all my life had I touched a trash bin, and now here I was hiding garbage up my sleeve. How repulsive! I 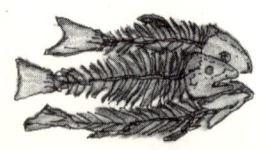could feel the cold herring scraps slipping down from the rolled hankie. There hadn't been time to find a better place to hide them, so there they were. Now I had to get out of this kitchen before the scaly, wet bundle fell out onto the floor.

"Look here, Clarissa Galloway," he said, smiling, "I've gotten quite used to seeing you roaming around up here, and 'tween decks,* and I've seen that odd carpetbag of yours. But picking through the trash box? Really!"

"Odd?" I snapped. "How dare you call me odd! We are complete strangers. You know nothing about me."

"Now wait a minute," he said. "First of all, I never called *you* odd. And secondly, my name is Eli. There, now we're no longer strangers."

"You'll forgive me," I said hotly, "but I never asked your name. So how is it that you know mine?"

"Well," he said, "everyone on board the *Wilmott* seems to know Dr. Galloway and his children. Your father has quite a following. Pretty clever doctor, if you ask me, to bring all his patients with him when he leaves town! Why, your President Henderson even told me that your father . . ."

"So that's it!" I said. "You're a snoop!" I began twisting my arm around as I spoke, hoping to wiggle the awful scraps back up my sleeve where I desperately needed them to stay. "No doubt you enjoy spying on a Britisher.* I've heard the Americans are famous for that!"

"Oh please," he laughed. "I only felt it was my duty as steward* to make certain the families are comfortable and well fed. Sometimes I must ask questions to find out, mustn't I?"

"Steward? Ha!" I smirked. "Why, you aren't old enough to be alone on this ship, never mind a steward."

Truly, I wasn't used to talking so rudely to anyone. I only hoped to make him angry enough to let me get away. But I could see he was thoroughly enjoying my distress. He answered with a smile.

"I've spent the last five years on board ships of one sort or another. Believe me, I know the work well. And it just so happens I will be seventeen in May."

I found it hard to believe that he was five years older than I. He *was* tall and appeared used to hard work. But his face was not rough and dark as the other sailors' faces were. I hated to admit it, but there was a kindness about his eyes that reminded me of my mother.

He began again. "Miss Galloway, I'm only concerned that you, your father, and brother are all right."

"Well," I said, "you needn't trouble yourself. My father is acquainted with the captain, and the Saints on this ship are well provided for. Now then, if you don't mind, I'll just be returning to my berth.* No doubt my father will be needing my help with Andrew."

I took a step toward him, hoping that by expecting him to move he would. He did not. He merely smiled down at me shaking his head and said, "What *are* you up to?"

I was struck with the notion to simply push past

him but knew that a lady would never do such a thing. And anyway, it would take more courage than I had after being caught in such a ghastly situation. "I've had quite enough of your questions," I said. "If you were any sort of gentleman, you would tend to your own affairs and let me by!"

He swiped off his blue sea cap with a flourish and bowed low, saying, "Why certainly, miss. I do beg your pardon!" Though he kept his head down, I could sense him chuckling under his breath.

I tossed my head back, and with one arm bent, so as to keep the smelly parcel from sliding out or up my arm, I strolled past with my chin held high. But before I was quite clear of him, my sleeve caught fast on a nail in the doorway. It yanked my arm backwards so hard that my hankie and its hidden fish heads plopped to the floor. They bounced and slid, finally stopping at the young man's feet. I stood horrified as he scooped up one of them with his bare hands and held it up to me.

"Well, well," he said, "and what have we here, little pelican?"

If he had any more to say, I'm sure I didn't hear it. With one remaining scrap in my hand, I ran.

CHAPTER THREE

A Secret Shared

I clamored up to the bunk box* where all my belongings were packed neatly in a bundle at one end. I was relieved to find that Andrew was still napping soundly on Father's side of the bed. It was my job to tend him during the day, and it wouldn't do to have him wake up alone. I found myself feeding and caring for Andrew pretty much on my own, but for once I really didn't mind.

Back home he would have been dragging me from one raft of trouble to another. But ever since our voyage began he had been shy and quiet, hanging behind me whenever anyone even spoke to him. This sailing business was so new that, while we could see the fascination on his face, he was still a bit fearful. Father said, "He's a hearty lad, and I fancy he will be his old noisy self soon enough, but for now we should just keep him in our sight."

I had truly expected it to be difficult to keep my little stowaway a secret. But from the beginning everyone was so busy getting organized, or dealing with seasickness, that after four days at sea no one—not even Andrew—was the wiser.

I pulled the carpetbag onto my lap and hurried to check my kitten. She slept warm in the flannel wrap, though she was breathing oddly. I lifted her out and laid her in the hammock of my skirt. She looked so thin and scraggly with her fur still dirty and matted. She was too weak to tidy it and I didn't dare bathe her while she was so ill. Unwrapping the fish morsel, I held it  up to her little gray nose. She blinked slowly and turned her head away.

"Please," I whispered, "just try a small taste. It will surely make you feel better. If only there were two drops of cream on this ship, I'd find a way to bring it to you. But I fear we won't be tasting cream, eggs, or anything really fresh and good for many weeks now. I suppose we'll be eating hard meat and rice until our teeth drop out. And if you knew how difficult a time I had smuggling you this! Why, I was nearly captured and tossed over the side by a terrible, meddling American boy."

Just then the wool blanket flew back and a curly brown head popped up.

"I say," whined the groggy little voice, "who you talking to, Clary?"

I threw my frock ruffles up and over the kitten curled in my lap. "Just having a bit of a chat with myself, to make sure I'm all right," I said, hoping he'd let it go. But he saw past my fib.

"Show me," he demanded. "Have you found a mouse?"

"Certainly not!" I said. "That's a dream of yours little man, not mine." Andrew climbed over the parting board* and scooted next to me. He leaned over and began to tug at my sleeve.

"A fish then," he said. "Has one of those sailors caught you a fish?"

"Andrew, stop it," I said, half turning my back to him. "If I had a fish in my lap I'd be tossing it out, not speaking to it. Now let's hop down and I'll find you a biscuit."

"No," he said, "I heard you. You were talking to your lap. I want to see what you got." He pulled at my hand and then began tugging the ruffle away. "Show me, show me, show me, show me . . ." he chanted.

"Ahhhh, boy!" I growled. "Can't you see when a person has a secret they'd like to keep?" He just looked up with round eyes, waiting. "It's no use," I sighed, moving the cloth just enough to give him a glimpse. Then I quickly covered her back up.

"Whoooo, Clary!" He looked down, then up into my face. "Where'd you get the rat?"

"Shhh! Andrew, are you daft?* This is not a rat, it's Lillibeth."

"Why's she so still?" he asked, looking more curious than worried. "She dead?"

"Of course she's not dead. Though she nearly was. Part drowned, I'd say. Anyway, I've got her now and we mustn't tell Father."

"Why not? Father is kind enough."

"Yes, I know, but . . ." I wasn't sure what to say. Father didn't like secrets. "It's just that I don't think kittens go well on passenger ships. Listen, she sleeps in my bag, so she won't be in the way." I wrapped her well and laid her back in carefully on top of my one good dress. "See?" I said. "We've just got to keep her warm and let her get well. Can I trust you to help me then?"

Andrew put his hand up and said solemnly, "May I boil in oil if I tell what I know!"

17

"Andrew!" I scolded. "Where'd you hear such talk?"

He smiled. "Father took me up on deck yesterday to hear the sermon. Brother Giles was talking a fearful long time, so I went looking about."

"You know full well that you've been warned not to wander topside alone," I said. "Something could happen. I heard Sister Miller say people get washed overboard all the time."

"Well, I found a piece of rope all tied to a post. I couldn't untie it. I did try. It was a splendid rope. Just then, a big man with gold anchors in his ears came along."

"Anchors in his ears—how dreadful!" I said, giving my brother a sour look.

"Gold ones, I tell you." He was thrilled at my disgust. "Anyway, he picked me straight up and said, 'The last mate what picked at me riggin'* was boiled in oil and flung out with the wash,'" he mimicked in a gruff voice.

"Oh, poor Andrew!" I shuddered. "Weren't you afraid?"

"Oh yes, terribly," he said, "but just then a tall boy came. Told the sailor it was a bad day for a swim. Before I had my feet under me, they were laughing and slapping each other's backs."

"Boy? What sort of boy?"

"Just a boy. Tall though, and light haired. Gave me a sweet and told me to go find my sister. So I did."

I pursed my lips, suspiciously. "Hmmm, let's go up and get some fresh air." I tried to help Andrew down, but he didn't need it. Under my breath I muttered, "Wretched spies."

CHAPTER FOUR

Topside

"Shield your eyes, Andrew," I said, "until they adjust to the brightness." Coming up on deck from our dark, muggy berth below always took a few minutes to get used to. But finally being able to throw our heads back and breathe fresh sea air was nearly as good as passing the baker's shop on bread day.

Aunt Polly used to say that March comes in like a lion, but the pleasant sea wind ruffling through my hair felt more like June. Closing my eyes, I held my face up to the soothing warmth of the sky. The great, heavy sails above us sounded like a flock of huge birds flapping past. But to see them reminded me of wash lines full of sparkling white bedclothes drying in the breeze.

The deck was alive with people, both young and

old, soaking in the sunlight. Children were playing close to their parents, as no one younger than ten was allowed topside alone.

On one side sat Brother Samuels and his son Johnny having a game of chess. It was great fun watching them grab at pieces, which, thanks to the sea, would slide along the board all by themselves.

Then there was Father's dear friend, President Henderson, a short, plucky little man, with the usual crowd around him, giving an afternoon sermon. Many of the elders and other leaders took turns speaking to the branch at regular meeting times, but our president needed only a simple question in order to begin his preaching.

This kind man had known the Prophet Joseph and been his close friend before the martyrdom, so his stories held everyone spellbound. Andrew and I stopped often to hear him because he took great pleasure in speaking so that even the young children could understand. As he spoke, it was easy to imagine what the Prophet was really like. It made it easier to remember why we were coming to America in the first place. He nodded and smiled as we passed.

We walked carefully along, holding any rail, rope,

or siding we could reach. Although today the sea was beautiful—silver and glimmering—the ship's own rocking made it hard for us to know where our feet would land. Until each passenger acquires his sea legs,* it feels almost as if one leg is just a bit shorter than the other. In fact, the children could keep the adults amused by losing their balance and ending up in a pile on what seemed to be a perfectly calm day.

We sat back against a row of planking and shared the bread and raisins from my canvas satchel. The food on board the *Wilmott* wasn't as bad as I had heard it could be. The steward brought us supplies as often as we needed them, and there was plenty of vinegar to freshen the drinking water. Father even had a small box of "extras" packed from our own cupboard—pickles, jams, and sweet currants.

Once we were underway, Father and a few others passed out roasted potatoes and oat bread, for it was the only thing the seasick stomachs could take and be grateful for. He and President Henderson had spent the first three days begging people up from their beds to the fresh air. Those that came on deck began to feel well enough to eat. But the more stubborn were even now still below and suffering. Father said by tomorrow he'd carry them up himself, willing or not, if they wouldn't come for their own good. "Giving in to seasickness," he said, "would bring on the fever, in record time."

We'd been lucky, Andrew and I, and had only felt badly for the first two days. President Henderson said that ofttimes children are so anxious to be up and doing that their insides never seem to notice the roll of the ship or the sea beneath it, while the adult stomach feels every wave.

Just then the captain, a seemingly jolly, tall fellow with a ruddy red beard, walked briskly past. He seemed to enjoy the people on board as if they all had been his friends from long ago. His loud voice boomed across the deck as he called out orders to his shipmates.

"When I'm a man," Andrew said, placing raisins carefully on the edge of his biscuit, "I expect to be a great sailor like Captain Larsen and sail clean around the world."

"Do you now?" I said, hardly listening. "And what will Father think of that?"

Andrew smiled, "Father will say, 'Go boy, and bring me back a coconut tree to plant in our garden, and I shall have shavings for my porridge.' As for me, I will have a little monkey from Africa in a great wooden cage."

23

"Big plans, Andrew. And what will you bring back for me, I wonder?"

"I'll go far, far away and find you a teacup and saucer, like mother's, with pink petals on it. Then, when you're sad and tired you can take a sip of broth from it and be warm and cheerful again."

"Oh, Andrew," I sighed, putting my arm around my brother. He suddenly seemed to be more grown-up than I'd realized. "That will be a good day. Thank-you."

Just then, from the stairwell came a shriek which turned every head.

"Edward!" With both hands gripping the stair rail, up came Sister Cooper. "Edward!" she wailed. "Where are you now? Fool man."

Sister Cooper and her husband, Edward, had been some of Father's first converts to the Church, over four years ago. They were a sweet old couple with very little of anything to spare, so whenever they needed Father's medical help they had often paid him with eggs, butter perhaps, or even a chicken.

It was only a month ago that Sister Cooper had come wanting paregoric* for her Edward and paid Father with a tiny gray kitten. He brought it home to me in his pocket, saying, "This one will need some

24

plumping up. I'm sure you can see to it." Two days later Brother Cooper had died.

Sister Cooper's mind didn't take the news well, and she had spells when she didn't seem to know he was gone at all. Making my way to her side, I linked her arm with my own. "Sister Cooper," I said, "come sit with Andrew and me. We're having bread and raisins."

"No, child," she cried. "I've lost Edward again. He went out to fetch some strawberries from the garden, but he's not come back."

"Strawberries?" Andrew said, his eyes getting big. "Who's got strawberries?"

"Shhhh, Andrew, no one's got them," I whispered. "Let it go."

"It's been hours, I tell you, hours. Edward! Where are you?" Sister Cooper cried.

"Come sit down, Sister Cooper," I said, pulling her gently. She dabbed at her eyes with a handkerchief, then blew her nose loudly. Crouching down she looked under the benches and around the corners we passed. She seemed not to even realize we were on a ship. Then, not knowing what else to say I blurted out, "Don't worry. We will find him."

"Ha!" Andrew giggled. "I'd like to see you."

"Qui-et," I said through my teeth. Lucky for us both that Sister Cooper was hard of hearing. I cleared my throat and and tried to keep a straight face, saying, "Why look, here's Sister Miller waiting to see you."

At last she sighed and plopped down next to the familiar group. Sister Miller had taken care of her elderly mother for seventeen years, and she smiled up at us. "There, there now Bessie," she said patting Sister Cooper's hand, "come have a rest now. We will all go in for supper soon enough." Then turning to me she said, "Run along, dear. I'll see to her. Oh, and tell the doctor thank you again. Good man, your father."

The heads in the small crowd began to nod and we heard several "Ayes" and a "Thank him for us, as well."

"Why," I said, "I didn't even know that you all had been ill."

The whole group roared with laughter, but I couldn't tell at what. With a polite curtsy, I took Andrew's hand and off we went.

CHAPTER FIVE

Good Advice

"I believe she's worse tonight, Andrew," I said. "Look at her, all skinny and limp." I'd been soaking dried kippers* in my small water tin hoping Lillibeth would get some good from it, but she seemed to be too tired and weak to drink much.

"Clary," Andrew pled, "let me find Father. He'll know how to set her right."

"No, Andrew. What if cats aren't allowed on board? Father could get in terrible trouble. And then what? One of those old sailor friends of yours might just throw her overboard for good luck!" Andrew looked hurt. I hadn't meant to raise my voice. Softly this time I said, "We'll just have to think of something else."

Just then I heard laughter coming from near the hatchway. Sister Miller was sharing any cheery news she could conjure up with everyone passing by.

I laid Lillibeth back in the carpetbag and covered her with my good shawl. Throwing back the makeshift curtain, I said, "Come along, Andrew, let's go visiting." We slid down and worked our way toward the long bench Sister Miller was resting on.

"Sister Miller, I was just wondering . . ."

"Yes, child?" she said.

"What I mean to say is, back home you had a lot of animals didn't you?"

"Aye, dear. Half dozen milking cows. But you've been to my place haven't you?"

"Yes, ma'am. It's just that, I'm trying to remember. Did you happen to have any smaller animals—say a dog or perhaps a cat?"

"Why dear me, yes," she laughed, "we had nine. Cats that is. Helpful with the mice. No dogs though. Why do you ask?"

"Well my brother and I were just wondering. Suppose one of your cats became ill, wouldn't eat and had a hard time breathing. Sleeping all the time. Maybe even had consumption."*

"Consumption?" she shuddered. "Whooo, well, everyone knows a cat will sleep a lot and refuse food while she is on the mend. But if she had consumption, I suppose I'd let her go."

"What do you mean by 'let her go?'" I winced.

"Child, there just isn't time to coddle all the runts and sickly creatures when there is a farm to run. The fit ones live and the weak ones don't is all I'm getting at. I wouldn't know how to treat a cat with consumption because I'd probably never do it."

"I see," I said, keeping my eyes on the floorboards. Andrew nudged me aside.

"A big animal then," he said. "A cow."

"Well now, an earning animal is another matter. My Daniel, rest his soul, was known to stay up all night with an ailing cow, doing heaven knows what. I was lucky not to have to handle the large animals much. I'm sorry children, I really can't say."

"Perhaps I can help you," came a familiar voice from behind. "Pardon me, but I couldn't help overhearing."

I could feel my face turning red, but I could not make myself look up.

"Thank goodness, Eli," said Sister Miller, "I'm so glad to see you. I've been meaning to have you fetch me a pint more vinegar. Mine is out."

"Right away, ma'am," he said, touching his cap. Sister Miller walked toward her bunk, leaving Andrew and me to deal with the American.

Turning to me, Eli said, "I'm very fond of animals myself. In fact, I have even pulled several through illness. If you will just tell me what you need."

"I don't know what you mean," I said, trying to avoid the smile he'd used the last time we met.

"Look," he whispered, "why don't you stop pretending and let me help you?"

"Tell him, Clary," Andrew said. "Maybe he *can* help."

"No," I whispered through clenched teeth.

"All right then, but I've brought you this." He pressed a small bundle into my hand. "You dropped it earlier."

"What is it?" I asked suspiciously.

"Only the lady's hankie." Eli smiled at me then turned to Andrew. Placing his hand on my brother's shoulder he said, "Tell your pretty sister not to be so stubborn. Some Americans can be trusted." He looked up at me and winked. Just then the eight o'clock prayer bell sounded. With that, he was gone.

The branch members began filing down the stairway in a slow steady line. Father was nearly the last one in. Catching my eye he worked his way through the crowd toward us. The children were hushed as President Henderson began speaking.

"My dear brothers and sisters. In faith, we couldn't have had more splendid weather if we had set it up ourselves."

"I've missed you two," Father whispered. "Where have you been hiding?"

"You're a fine one to speak," I scolded. "*I've* been in plain sight all day. We did begin to wonder if *you'd* washed over the side, though."

Father laughed.

"Shhhh!" Andrew nudged us. "Prayers." Father snatched off his hat and bowed his head.

Brother Adams offered a lovely, short prayer that the wind would blow us safely to Zion. "Amen," we echoed.

"Have you eaten at all tonight, Father?"

"Picked up a scrap or two round about."

"Come now," I said. "I'll fetch you some supper."

We made our way back to the bunks and Father hoisted Andrew up to his space with little effort. Some of the adults began bedding down the younger children, and many settled themselves in as well. One by one nearly half of the lanterns were put out. With the hatchway lanterns remaining lit each night, it never became completely dark.

"So," Father said, "what have we in our kitchen

tonight? I haven't been careful to come at our own cooking time. I fear I've left my little family to do for themselves. Are you making out all right?"

"Oh yes, Father," I said. "Our group has chosen Brother Kirby to cook for us."

Each Monday the stewards would hand out a week's worth of provisions to the head of every household. Before breakfast our group's cook would post the day's menu. It would be each family's responsibility to get the necessary supplies to him and he would cook it all at once.

"In return for his keeping us so well fed we've all agreed to tend his two babies," I replied.

"Yes. It has been a struggle for him to make this trip with no wife to care for the children." He pulled Andrew's nightshirt into place, as the boy was falling asleep with only one arm in. Father then spread the wool coverlet over him.

I filled his plate with dried kippers and a chunk of bread and cheese. He ate gratefully without speaking.

"You look tired, Father. There isn't much sickness on board now is there?"

"No. I do expect to have a good sleep tonight. But I'll be up on deck for awhile yet with the brethren."

"I'm glad, Father. I enjoy the singing. I shall be listening for your voice."

He touched my hair and kissed me before returning above. Blowing out our lantern, I slid into my nightgown and remembered the handkerchief still in my dress pocket. I reached into the carpetbag and stroked Lillibeth before settling down under the wool comforter.

The Saints on deck began singing, and as always, Father's voice went straight to my heart. I drifted off to sleep, hearing:

> *Farewell now to dear Britain,*
> *Thy children cast upon the sea*
> *Toward the outstretched arms of Zion*
> *Our hearts returning oft to thee.*

Chapter Six

The Brew

Sister Adams began feeling ill in the early morning hours, so Father took his bag and left before the six o'clock bell. He was fearful of her baby coming too soon.

"Oh, Father," I sighed when I noticed him gone, "missing cleanup again." But as I ventured up the stairs and carefully emptied the wastebin over the side, I felt someone take my arm. Startled, I pulled away and turned. It was Eli.

"You again," I said. "Some people seem to be everywhere."

"Small ship," he smiled. "Here, I've made you some broth. Don't let the smell fool you. It should help."

"Why?" I asked, "I'm not ill."

"Clarissa," he said, "it's not for you, so don't drink it." Leaning over he whispered, "It may just save your little stowaway. I'll check on you later."

I stood there with my mouth open, holding the steaming cup, as Eli ran back down the stairs.

"It does smell dreadful," I said aloud, though grateful to have help of any kind.

Below, Andrew was already dressed and trying to stack the blankets. "Here, let me help you," I said. I began folding when Andrew's groan stopped me. He was holding the cup to his lips.

"If this is my breakfast, I'm not having any. It smells bad and tastes badder still."

"I don't suppose it will kill you, but it isn't your breakfast. It's Lillibeth's. Though, I fear she won't take it."

After pouring a small amount into the tin platter, I held it out to her. She sniffed first, then began lapping slowly at the green-gray broth.

"She likes it!" Andrew said. "It's high time she ate something. I don't think her nose works though. It's clear she can't smell it."

"I believe she wants more," I said as I refilled the platter, this time to the rim. She emptied it a second time.

When she had finished, I held her up against my cheek and whispered, "Please get well." Her breathing still sounded rattily, but I was relieved to know she had something warm inside her. Then tucking her away again in the dark cave of my bag, I said, "You just rest now. Come Andrew, we'd best see what Brother Kirby needs from our rations to make breakfast."

We both ran up the stairs and straight to the galley doorway. Brother Kirby was already working hard at the stove, stirring a thick batter.

"Why, Sister Galloway," he said, "have you come for your meal so soon?"

"Yes, sir. I mean, no, sir," I said. "Brother Kirby, we missed hearing what was to be for breakfast today. Are we too late to bring you our supplies?"

"Dear me, no," he said, his eyes twinkling. "I'm feeling a bit adventurous and believe I'll try my hand at griddle cakes. We have all the right things for it here in the kitchen. Now if the ship doesn't rock them off the griddle we'll be fine."

I smiled at Andrew. "Griddle cakes!" I said. "What a relief it will be to have something different than crackers and fish this morning."

"I'm sure it's not what a fine lady like yourself is used to," Brother Kirby said, "but I'll do my best. If only there was a spot of treacle* or preserves. We'd be at the Queen's table, that's what!"

Raising my eyebrows and nudging Andrew, we raced back down to our cubbyhole. Giggling, we pulled the long box from behind our supply barrel and untied the rope around it. The shiny bottles seemed to sparkle in the lamplight. We lifted each jar from the straw packed around it until we found a dark one marked "plum preserves—1855."

"Only one year old," I said.

Andrew found a small can of golden syrup and hollered, "Hurray!"

"I'll carry the glass," I said, "and you bring the tin. Won't Brother Kirby be surprised?"

Andrew's face clouded. "Wait. If we take this up, it won't come back, will it?"

"There's more. And anyway, Father would be pleased to know we are sharing."

He walked slowly behind me as we climbed back up to the sunlight. By now, there was a line forming from the kitchen, but when the members saw our treasures they patted and pushed us up to the front. Brother Kirby turned with two cakes on his long, flat knife. Instead of holding out our plates to him, we held up our sweets.

"Oh, well now," Brother Kirby beamed, "you two have been to heaven and back this morning haven't you? Everyone will certainly envy your breakfast."

"Brother Kirby," I said, "surely you don't think we'd eat this alone. We've brought it for the table."

Andrew stood shaking his head and scowling, holding his can tightly to his chest.

"Haven't we, Andrew?" I said firmly. Andrew puffed a sigh and held out the can. Brother Kirby threw back his head and laughed so hard that the cakes tumbled to the floor.

"Ahhh, children," he said, "the apple doesn't fall far from the tree, does it?"

"Pardon, sir?" I said.

"It does an old heart good to see two children who can be as generous and kind as their father. He must be very proud of you." Then piling four cakes each on our tin plates he said, "Go eat and be the honored guests at the table." He rumpled Andrew's hair and we took our plates below. The meal was cheerful and lively as the sweets were passed around to all the members of our little branch. The children giggled and licked their fingers as they ate. Old Sister Cooper went out to find her Edward so he wouldn't miss the treat. Even Andrew seemed pleased at making so many people happy at one sitting, though when the meal was done, his precious tin was emptied and tossed to the wastebin.

Later, while returning from a sunbath on deck, Andrew and I found another steaming cup of the foul broth. The old one had been taken away. A small scrap of paper by the side of it read:

I see someone liked the brew—
hope it wasn't your brother.
Chin up, Pelican!

Eli

CHAPTER SEVEN

Father's Fur Coat

"Hey, what?" Father yelled. The sun couldn't be up yet, but Father so rarely ever raised his voice that Andrew and I both sat straight up in bed at once.

"Are you dreaming, Father?" Andrew asked, rubbing his eyes.

"I believe I must be, son," he said. "A nice, warm dream of wearing a soft fur coat around my neck. Clarissa, would you be so good as to explain this?"

I stared hard, straining to make my eyes work in the darkness. Father's large hand was held out straight towards me. When I was finally awake enough to make out the shape in Father's hand, I discovered what Andrew already knew. My brother sat staring, holding his hand over his mouth. Father was gripping a purring, contented Lillibeth.

"Well, Clarissa?" he asked.

"Oh dear," was all I could squeeze out. I desperately

wished for a light, to see if Father was taking this well, or if I was in real trouble. Lifting her gently from Father's hand, I noticed that Lillibeth wasn't acting at all limp or sickly. In fact, when I placed her in my lap, she jumped back out and began playfully swiping at my fingers. She rolled over on her back kicking and chewing the coverlet. For a moment I forgot Father and squealed, "She's well, Andrew! She's well! And we thought there was no hope."

I heard the hiss of the lantern as Father lit it and swung it on to the post hook. I looked into his face hoping to find the patience he was known for.

There he sat, staring at me, waiting. Andrew and I worked our way back and forth through the story, telling it from beginning to end. Our words sped up toward the finish, hoping Father would understand and not be angry.

After a long silence and much chin rubbing, he finally spoke. "Well, children, I suppose you felt you had no choice. And I see your hearts were in the right place. However, I do wish you had told me at the start."

"Oh, we couldn't, Father," I said. "We were just certain she'd be tossed over and you'd be in trouble with the captain."

"Darling," he said, holding me by the chin, "the captain is a fine fellow and has a cat of his own. I don't expect he will mind at all knowing Lillibeth is with us."

"Don't tell him, Father," I pled.

"Yes, I shall tell him, and we will be completely honest from this moment on." Father reached out and hugged me, smashing a sleepy Andrew in the middle. "It will be fine, trust me. And in the meantime, let's have no more secrets between us, shall we?"

"Yes, Father," I sighed, lying back on my mattress. What a relief it was to no longer be keeping anything from him.

After breakfast, I skipped up on deck and found Father in a circle with President Henderson, Captain Larsen, and a few others. As I approached, the captain bellowed, "Come girl, you needn't be afraid of an old tar like me!" I looked shyly around Father and stepped forward. "I'm told by my friend here that you are in possession of a stowaway," he said.

"Ahhh, yes sir," I said. "Only I didn't mean . . ."

"I see no reason for concern. There is plenty to eat on this ship, even for cats. As long as you keep her below deck, she can roam about as she pleases. In fact, before this voyage is over she may be old enough to earn her keep down in the hold.* Perhaps she'll find the rats to her liking. I just hope they aren't bigger than she is!"

"Oooh," I said, under my breath. The men laughed.

Just then Eli appeared. "Your coffee, sir," he said. He smiled and tipped his cap at me. "Clarissa."

"I see you two know each other," Captain Larsen said.

"Oh yes, sir," Andrew piped up. "Eli gave us the medicine that saved Lillibeth."

"Is that so, Eli?" the captain said, his mouth breaking into a sideways grin. "Then perhaps you wouldn't mind helping this young lady find a crate for her kitten to sleep in."

"Kitten is it?" Eli smirked. "Yes, sir. Right away."

Andrew, Eli, and I started quietly down the stairs toward the hold. The silence was uncomfortable, so at last I said, "Listen, I haven't had a chance yet to thank you for helping us. It was very kind of you."

"There's no need to thank me," he said. "It was my pleasure."

"Also," I said, chewing my lip, "I'd like to apologize for the way I acted that day in the galley. It was just so terrible being caught in such a predicament."

Eli chuckled. "Actually, I rather enjoyed watching you squirm!"

"I'm so embarrassed," I said, dropping my eyes. "You must have thought I was behaving like such a fool."

Sitting on an old trunk, he took off his cap and combed his fingers through his hair. "On the contrary, I learned long ago that people aren't always what they seem to be."

I nodded. "You did save Lillibeth's life with that broth of yours."

Andrew wrinkled his nose. "Tastes nasty, though. I never thought she'd take a lick."

"Animals are amazing," Eli said. "They can often sense what will make them well and usually show more brains than humans about taking it. So, she's better then? Lillibeth, is it?"

"Yes," I said. "She's romping and playing and nearly her old self again. So how is it, you being a sailor, that you know about animals?"

"It's this way," he said. "My mother died when I was born. And my father was never one to stay anyplace for long. So, I was raised by my grandparents, on their ranch in Vermont. It was there that I learned how to care for animals. My grandparents died when

I was eleven, so seeing little ahead of me, I went to sea. If I had a choice now though, I'd go back and try farming."

"Then you don't care for sailing?"

"I like it well enough. But someday, I'd like to have my own place. Raise sheep maybe, and corn." Eli looked off with that same glimmer that touched Father's eyes when he spoke of Zion. "Sometimes, when we come to port and everyone gets off with their trunks and bundles, heading West," he looked away, "well, I envy them."

"I suppose I'd have been happy to stay in England all my life. My mother is buried there, and we left behind all but a few of our things. Father says we are going to America to build up the kingdom, and we should not try to count the cost."

"Yes, I know something about the Mormons," Eli said. "This ship has carried thousands to America, but it is an easier and more pleasant journey when the passengers are Saints, as you call them."

"How do you mean?" I asked.

"Well, for one thing, there is more friendship and cooperation among your people. And everyone seems to be more tidy and conscientious. There are men like your father, who never seem to notice whether someone is rich or poor, passenger or crew. And though I don't understand it, there even seems to be less sickness among Mormons. It's a curious group you travel with, Clarissa Galloway."

I smiled. It was nice being thought well of by this young man. And I was proud to be traveling with a group of people who were different simply because they tried to be kind and good.

Suddenly, a curly head banged up through the pile of crates. "Will this do?" Andrew said, holding up an old box the size of an apple crate.

"Splendid," I said. "It will be just perfect."

CHAPTER EIGHT

Lost at Sea

All morning the captain stood on deck staring quietly off toward the horizon. He appeared to be looking at something the rest of us couldn't see.

"Clary," Andrew said, "what's he spying?"

"Perhaps an island, or another ship. I don't know." Occasionally the first mate would stand beside him. They would point out at the sea, speak in low voices, and nod to each other.

The wind was a bit gusty as Andrew and I stood looking out at the same sea. The white-tipped waves slapped the side and splashed up on deck.

"Whooo!" I said. "I don't mind dampness so much, but I don't care to be soaked down. Let's go below and see if Father is back yet."

The ship began to rock and plunge with greater force. Andrew and I sat quietly on our bunk, listening as the creaking of the timbers grew louder and louder.

Finally Andrew wailed, "I'm afraid. Where's Father?"

"He's bound to be along soon," I said, patting Andrew's hand, all the while wondering to myself where Father was.

The Saints had all scurried below as the sea became more and more unpleasant. For the little ones it was the most difficult, as each time they stood, they were knocked off their feet again. Most just stayed sitting on their beds. At last the first mate came below and gave us the word. In a stiff, nervous voice he said loudly, "The captain has ordered the hatchways* sealed. A walloping gale is approaching at a tremendous speed. All passengers are hereby advised to return to quarters and remain below for the duration."

All passengers? I thought. Climbing down from the bed and holding to the posts as I went, I reached the mate, who was busy giving instructions to President Henderson. I cleared my throat and said, "If you please, sir."

"Not now, missy," he said. "You'd best be for tying down your belongings or they will be hitting the other end of the ship."

"But, sir," I pled, "My father, Dr. Galloway, is not back yet. Have you seen him?"

President Henderson put his hand on my shoulder saying, "Now don't you worry, Clarissa. He's not gone far. I'll check on him and be right back down." He gave me a reassuring glance, nodded to the mate, and went through the door. I went back to my bed, and found the blankets all a shambles.

"Really, Andrew! It's not even close to nap time. Look, President Henderson has promised to hunt out Father so you needn't be afraid." Our belongings began sliding at the side of the bed. I blew out our lantern to lower the risk of fire. "Andrew, help me tie down our things or we'll lose them." I pushed the blankets with my foot. A startled Lillibeth scampered out of the rumpled covers and bounced off the bed. I quickly patted down the blankets until they were flat. No Andrew.

"Andrew!" I said firmly, in case he thought hiding from me would be clever. No answer. My heart began to pound. "Andrew!" I shouted. The ship rocked as though it would tip clear onto its side and pour us all out. Then it would right itself and begin tilting the other way. Babies were crying. Little children squealed when they were thrown off their beds. Those who hadn't tied down their possessions were now forced to watch helplessly as they rolled from one side of the room to the other.

I pulled myself from post to post, ducking lanterns and buckets. I asked everyone if they had seen my brother, but no one had. Just then Father appeared looking relieved to see me. "There you are, love," he said. "Bad storm upon us. Where's your brother?"

Grabbing his arm I said, "I can't find him!"

"What are you saying?"

"I've asked everyone." But Father didn't wait to hear any more. Pushing past me he lunged toward the hatchway and took the stairs three at a time. I slid down against the post and began to cry. I should have stayed with Andrew! Why wasn't I watching him?

I sat with my arms gathered around my knees sobbing until Father returned, wild-eyed.

"They've closed us in!" he said frantically. He chewed his knuckle, then banged his fist on the table. "My boy!" he cried. "Not even to be able to search!" He covered his face with his hands. Putting my arm around his back I tried to comfort him. But we both knew the dangerous truth. A five-year-old boy stood no chance on deck in a storm. Grown men could be washed over the side in an instant.

Suddenly a voice came out of the darkness. "Is there trouble here, Dr. Galloway? Can I help you?" There stood Eli, with more securing rope.

Father turned and grabbed him by the coat with both hands.

"My boy! He's lost! I beg you to let me go above to find him!"

"You mustn't, sir." Eli said. "Only seasoned men are allowed above. The minute you opened the hatch you'd be pushed back down. Why *I'm* not even supposed to come on deck," he paused. "It's for your own safety, sir."

"But what of my Andrew? He's only a child!" Father begged. Eli shook his head helplessly.

Putting my head back down into my hands, I whispered, "Please, Heavenly Father, help us. Don't let us lose our little Andrew."

Eli took a deep breath and squared his shoulders. "I'll search for him, sir," he said. "I won't come back without him." He swung open the latch and pulled himself through. Water poured in running streams across the floor, until the wind slammed the hatch shut behind him.

"Come now, Clarissa," Father said softly. His voice was hoarse and his hand on my shoulder trembled. "We'll tie down what's left of our things and wait."

"How can we stand it, Father?" I cried.

"We will have faith and trust in the Lord. It's all we

can do." Wiping at the tears on my face, I helped Father stack our things and secure them to the posts.

Holding onto our bunks for what seemed like hours, we waited. The thunder was deafening. The women began to whimper. In my terror I imagined a giant hand pressing down at the bow* of the ship and playfully releasing it only to plunge down even harder on the stern.* The room which had been so warm and happy for all these weeks had become dark and chilling. I covered my ears to stop the noise which pounded through the room. It seemed as though some force was trying to tear our little ship into pieces and scatter us to the four winds.

Water and wind blew in upon us, as the hatch was pulled open from the outside. A tall figure appeared in the shadows, making his way down the stairs. As he came nearer and approached the lamplight, I could barely make out the dripping wool cap. In a second I saw it was Eli carrying my brother.

"Father!" I shouted.

He was ahead of me, bounding off the bunk and taking the two into his arms. Tearing a wet, tired Andrew from his rescuer, Father hugged and kissed him, crying, "My boy, my boy!"

I ran to Eli without thinking and threw my arms

around his neck. Then remembering myself I pulled away. Looking down I whispered, "Thank you."

Eli smiled and his face took on a moment of color, then, turning he said, "Sir, after all you've done for your people and the crew, I'm pleased to have the chance to help you."

Father laid Andrew on the bed, wiping the wet hair out of his face. There above his left eye was a nasty looking purple bump. "What happened to you, son?" Father said. Andrew didn't answer.

"I feared, sir, that he'd gone over the side. But then I got it in my head to search below. The thunder, luckily, frightened him from the deck down to the hold. The way the crates were being tossed I suppose would explain the bruise. I hope he will be all right."

"We will take him," Father laughed, "even battered a bit. He leaned over and said, "Won't we, son?" Andrew nodded wearily.

Wrapped up in relief, we hadn't noticed that the buckets had stopped swinging, the crying had hushed, and the people were nearly all asleep. There in the darkness, wet and exhausted, the warmth began to return.

CHAPTER NINE

The Fever

"Now then," I said. "We left Liverpool on Tuesday, March fourth, so that means we've been on this ship fifty-six days." Andrew nodded. "And in that time, we've seen forty-two seabirds, counted fifteen flying fish, played thirteen games of checkers . . ."

"Which I won mostly," Andrew said.

"Hush, I'm not finished. Read seven books, attended nineteen sermons, and thanks to Lillibeth's keen eye helped dispose of three rats, the wretched things."

"Don't forget, we've eaten at least a thousand pounds of hardtack."*

"Yes, we won't miss those old biscuits."

Sitting in the sun holding our basket, we waited for the crowd at the supply room to die down. The remaining rations were being divided up among the passengers. Our voyage was nearly over and we would be in Boston Harbor soon. Everyone had gathered with their crates and barrels to carry back whatever would be given to them.

"Let's get in line now," I said. "It's thinned out a bit." We pulled our basket along as the line inched forward. I was happy to see that Eli and two sailors were at the door of the supply room. They were handing out bundles of flour, meal, biscuits, and other leftover items.

"Use what you can," the captain had said, "the rest is fish food."

"At last," Andrew sighed as our turn came. We pushed our basket in front of us, while the sailors tossed the packages in until they piled up. Eli turned with his arms full and smiled. His face was gray and weary and his blonde hair looked damp and disheveled. It appeared as though he'd been up all night, yet his voice was kind and cheerful.

"I've orders," he said, "to ask each passenger if there is anything else you're in need of."

"Hmmmm," I said slyly, "You wouldn't happen to have a nice fresh *peach* in that closet would you?"

"I'm sorry, ma'am," he teased, "just gave the last one away. Afraid you missed it." He took off his cap and wiped his forehead. "But wait," he said, "I do have a surprise."

"You do?" I asked, "What is it?"

He reached into his coat pocket and held out . . .

"An orange!" I squealed. "Wherever did you get it?"

"Last night after midnight we passed another vessel. If the captains are chums, the ships are steered close enough to swap news. As a joke, we threw our old moldy bread onto their deck, saying, 'Get used to this, fellows!' They tossed us half a dozen fresh oranges." Eli closed his eyes hard for a moment, then shook his head as if to wake himself up.

"Are you all right?" I asked.

"A bit tired, I think, is all. Now pelican, you'd better hide that fruit from the children or if I know you, it will all be shared away."

"I don't mind sharing. I feel badly eating treats in front of people who have gone without most of their lives. To my mind, it's a wonder they could make this voyage at all. I know it's taken nearly every penny *we* had to do it. And that was just for the three of us."

Eli looked puzzled. "Clarissa, your father is a wealthy man. He could take this trip ten times over and never notice."

"All I know is Father had been selling off our

things for weeks before we had enough money to book passage. It was only at the last minute I thought to take a handkerchief or I'd have nothing but the few clothes that would fit in my trunk. It must cost more than you know."

"You really don't understand, do you?" Eli said.

"Understand what?" The color had gone from his face, and his hair was dripping wet. "Eli, you don't look well."

"Clarissa," he said low, "none of these people would be here at all, if it weren't for your father." He gripped the barrel in front of him tightly.

"Eli, what is it?"

Andrew dropped the basket and ran to Eli, who teetered forward, his eyes distant. For a brief moment, he looked right into my face, then crumpled to the floor.

"Eli!" I screamed. "Help, someone! Help us!" Kneeling beside him, I dipped my handkerchief into the cool water from the barrel, and patted his face. "It's no use! He is burning up!"

Andrew came in with two sailors who had duty nearby.

"What's this?" the bearded one asked. "Eli's down!" he shouted to his shipmates. We stood back as a group gathered and the largest of them lifted Eli's limp body like a bag of apples.

"Where are you taking him?" I asked.

"We will see to him, miss. Have no fear."

I stood by helplessly, unable to think what to do. Stooping down to pick up the orange that had dropped unnoticed to the floor, my mind turned to Father.

I ran first to the sickbeds down below. When anyone had a fever or needed special care, Father had tended to them here so as not to risk the health of the other passengers. There were only three people in the beds now. Sister Mead was awake, so I ran to her side. "Please," I whispered, "I'm sorry to disturb you, but has my father been here?"

"Yes," she said weakly. "He has just left us. Called away."

"Did you hear where? Who called him?"

Sister Mead just shook her head and closed her eyes. I went back up on deck. No sign of him anywhere. Maybe someone needed him in the 'tween decks, I thought. Heading back to our bunks I found him packing his black medicine bag. I grabbed onto his arm "Oh Father, I'm so glad to see you."

I tried to catch my breath. "Please, you've got to

help Eli. He's terribly ill. The sailors have taken him away. He is burning up."

"Not Eli too!" Father sighed, shaking his head. "I can't come yet. I've been called to the captain's cabin."

"But Father, he's my friend. He may be dying!"

Taking me by the shoulders, he said, "Clarissa, I will come as soon as I can. In the meantime let's just pray it's not the fever, in either place."

I ran behind him, pleading as he wound through the corridors and up the stairs. He stopped and knocked on a large oak door which flew open at once. There stood Captain Larsen with the first look of fear I'd ever seen on his face.

"Come in, doctor," he said.

Father, taking his outstretched hand, said, "Captain, are you ill?"

"No, Dr. Galloway. It's my son!"

"Your son?"

"Please doctor, he hasn't much life left in him." Father stepped up to the side of the bed, with the captain behind him. I tried to see around them.

A large sailor took my arm, saying, "It's bad in here, miss. No place for a lady. You'd best run along."

"Father!" I called out. He stood staring down at the fellow on the large bed, then turned to me, shaking his head.

"Clarissa, get President Henderson quickly!"

As the captain stepped aside to let Father work, I saw the ghostly sick figure on the bed. My heart sank within me as I realized that the captain's dying son was Eli.

CHAPTER TEN

New Eyes

There was no sleep for me as I waited at the end of the corridor, alone in the dark. I'd been driven away by the captain himself, saying, "Go girl—lest your father finds his own child in such a state! It's not safe for you here."

President Henderson went in at Father's request and came out slowly, saying, "It's in the Lord's hands now."

Father said very little when he came out. He only mumbled to himself, "Typhoid. Most deadly." He leaned up against the wall and grabbed his hair. At last, he noticed me sitting exhausted, where I'd been all night.

"My poor girl," he said, taking me to my feet. "What a terrible fright you've had." We walked slowly through the aisles and down the stairway until we reached our own beds.

"Will he die, Father?" I asked softly. I thought of the broth Eli had conjured up weeks ago for Lillibeth and wondered if there wasn't some magic potion we could make now to save *his* life. "Is there no hope?"

"This fever is to be feared above all else. I've given him what little medicine there was. But while making him comfortable and tending to him, I could see that he was nearly gone. The captain stepped up most desperately and said, 'I've heard your people have a kind of power—power that can heal even a sickness such as this.'"

"I told him, 'If it's the Lord's will that he recover from this sickness and there is enough faith."

"Father, did you do it?" I cried. "Did you give Eli a blessing?"

"When President Henderson came we put our hands upon the lad. Curiously enough, I was impressed to tell him that his life would be spared if there was sufficient faith. I felt strongly that the Lord has great plans for him."

"Does that mean he will live?"

"Remember, if there is enough faith even mountains can be moved."

"Then we shall begin moving them at once."

"Imagine," Andrew said, "Eli being the captain's own son all this time and never telling us."

"Perhaps he just wanted us to like him for himself, not for who his father was," I said.

"Do you suppose we will see him before we leave?"

"Father says no. We will be in port by morning, and even though he will live, he is still too weak for visitors. I can't bear to think we will never see him again."

Our things were packed up, and by first light the land we'd longed for came into view. It held much less interest to me now as I thought of my friend still too sick to know how we'd miss him. I gathered my belongings into a bundle and filled my carpetbag with anything small enough to fit inside. I looked everywhere for my handkerchief but I must have lost it for good this time.

Lillibeth was much too big and impatient to fit in the bag now. Had she been smaller, she still wouldn't have agreed to go in quietly. Father had fashioned a crate with a heavy lid to keep her from running off once we had landed. She was not pleased and let me know it. Each time I walked past her, she slipped her paw through the wooden slats and took a swing at my skirt.

"Stop it now, you naughty thing," I said, working my finger through the slats to rub her head. "Won't it be good to finally be on solid ground? Then we'll see how you like it. You won't know how to behave." I pulled out a strip of dried beef and dropped it through to her, and she was content for a moment.

The members were busy with their stacks and piles, buttoning up children's coats and waiting to bring their things up on deck.

As I looked into the familiar faces around me, I saw young babies, old men, mothers, fathers, children, and grandparents. All from our very own town. I had been to nearly every one of these peoples' homes. Some I had come to know as well as I knew myself. It was such a blessing that we were all still together. What love had grown inside me for these members as I watched them every day doing ordinary things: wiping sticky chins, washing dishes, making up beds and saying prayers together.

Truly a miracle, I thought, that the way was provided for us all to come together. I looked over at

Sister Miller chatting with the Samuels family. "Yes, yes," she said, nodding slowly. "I even offered to be Dr. Galloway's housekeeper until our debt was paid back. He wouldn't hear of it. Said our passage was not a loan but a gift. To all of us."

"The way was provided," I whispered. Just then, a flood of thoughts rushed through my mind. Father saying, "We've fasted and prayed to stay together and the Lord has opened a way." Then Eli's words, "Pretty clever doctor to take all his patients with him." Brother Kirby saying, "as kind and generous as your father." And finally, the last words Eli had spoken to me, "None of these people would be here at all if it weren't for your father."

It was as if the sun was shining at last down in our dark little room. Could it be possible? Was it Father who paid the passage for these sixty-three people? Had I wasted time with sadness over leaving behind my own simple things when his only desire was to bring people? Our friends. No wonder he was thanked at every turn. No wonder Andrew and I were treated so kindly. No wonder Father was so loved!

Looking up again at the sweet faces around me, I realized we might never have seen them again, had my father been any other kind of man. With my heart full to bursting, I jumped up and ran above, looking over the whole deck until I found him. There he stood laughing and talking with a small crowd, watching the ship inch its way to the dock.

I couldn't contain the pride I felt at being his daughter. Running to his side, I threw my arms around him.

"Hold on there!" he cried, stumbling back.

"I love you so much, Father," I said.

Lifting my chin he laughed, "What's brought this on you, child?"

"I understand now that you were right. People are so much more important than things." Surprised at my outburst, the crowd laughed heartily. Father kissed the top of my head.

"So," he said, "are we ready for firm ground?" We watched the gangplank* being placed as people crowded to see the landing.

Just then the captain appeared from behind us, looking tall and stately in his dress coat.

"It's been a memorable voyage, Doctor Galloway. I'm in your debt."

"Read the book I gave you, sir," Father said, "and any debt to me will be paid."

Turning to me, Captain Larsen said, "And as for you miss, I hope you won't judge Eli too harshly. He's a good lad. But from the beginning, he has refused any special treatment. It's been his choice to work alongside the men. And a hard worker he is, too. Never a complaint, though I've known all the while that he longed to be someplace else."

I felt a jab at my heart, having heard weeks ago from Eli's own lips where that "someplace else" was.

"Now then," he said, taking my hand, "he'd have me give you this before you leave—a sort of good-bye token if you please." Then he gently folded my fingers around a tiny parcel secured with twine.

I smiled, hoping the color in my face didn't show the delight I felt at knowing that even now, as sick as he'd been, Eli had thought of me. I walked to the side rail, opened the wrapping, and found a small note written inside.

Dear Clarissa,

If there were only a few more days left, I'm sure I'd be well enough to tell you good-bye in person. I regret not seeing you before you go. My father tells me that your father saved my life—not so much with his pills as with a curious kind of blessing. At any rate, I thank him, and

you as well. The journey has been better with you here.
Who knows? Perhaps we will meet again someday.
Watch for me. I'll be heading west.

> *Your Friend,*
> *Eli Larsen*

P.S. Thank your father for the book. My father has
been reading it to me. Here is something for you to
remember me by. Eli

I slid off the string and unfolded the paper. There
within the wrappings was a tiny bird with beautiful
outstretched wings, carved from a white and pink
shell.

Andrew tugged at my sleeve. "Show me what you
got," he pestered. "Oooo, nice bird."

"Oh, it's not just a bird," I smiled. "It's a pelican."

GLOSSARY

In Clarissa's own words:

berth (pg. 12) On a ship, the bunk beds are sometimes called berths.

bow (pg. 52) The front of a ship is called the bow. The back is called the stern.

Britisher (pg. 11) Many Americans called people from England, Britts, British, or English. But we called ourselves Britishers.

bunk box (pg. 14) Our wooden bunk beds had sides which were built up higher than the straw-filled mattresses. This helped to keep us from rolling out of bed when the ship rocked.

consumption (pg. 28) Whenever someone had a sickness which made it difficult to breathe, we called it consumption. It may have really been pneumonia or tuberculosis.

daft (pg. 17) When someone is acting terribly silly or foolish, we call them daft.

galley (pg. 9) The kitchen on a ship. Usually a small room on deck with a stove and a table.

gangplank (pg. 66) A wooden walkway much like a bridge used to let people walk from the ship to the pier.

gold bible (pg. 5) Many people who didn't understand about the Book of Mormon, called it Joseph Smith's gold bible, because it is scriptures translated from plates of gold.

hold (pg. 43) Usually the very bottom deck of a ship. The storage room where trunks, luggage and cargo are kept.

hop it (pg. 6) When my father says, "Hop it!" I know he means hurry along.

house and home (pg. 4) In England, house and home are not the same thing. A house is the building where you live. A home is everything inside the house; the furniture and all your belongings.

kippers (pg. 27) A herring or other fish that has been dried or smoked or pickled.

laces and shawls (pg. 5) The doilies, table cloths, afghans and pretty, dainty things.

packet ship (pg. 2) Our ship was used to pack people and things back and forth across the sea. Some ships made the same voyage that we did six or seven times a year.

paregoric (pg. 24) A medicine used to help many illnesses, but especially stomachaches.

parting board (pg. 16) The long plank of wood used to separate one side of the bed from the other.

riggin' (pg. 18) The sailor meant to say rigging. The rigging is all the ropes, knots, and chains used to raise and lower the sails.

sea legs (pg. 22) Once a person gets used to living on a ship rolling through the sea, he barely notices it moving. They call it having your sea legs.

stern (pg. 52) The rear of a ship is called the stern. The front is called the bow.

steward (pg. 11) A member of the ship's crew who sees to everyone's needs and problems.

treacle (pg. 36) A sticky, sweet syrup, much like molasses.

'tween decks (pg. 10) The deck below the top and above the hold is called 'tween decks because it is between the decks. We slept and ate most of our meals here.

What Really Happened

Between the years 1840 and 1900 The Church of Jesus Christ of Latter-day Saints grew from roughly 25,000 members to 183,144 worldwide. It is particularly fascinating to note that of the 89,000 new members who immigrated to America, over 48,000 came from Great Britain alone.

It is said that when a visitor passed through the Salt Lake valley in 1860 they would have left believing that this was indeed a British church. For by this time nearly every household had at least one member with a strong English accent.

Not only from England, but from dozens of countries they came, leaving behind all they knew and loved to gather with the Saints and respond to the Prophet's call: Come to Zion.

About the Author

Launi K. Anderson was raised in Los Angeles and San Diego, California. She worked for a large local bookstore for four years and became the children's book buyer. She loves historical fiction and enjoys the research as much as the writing.

Her favorite things are: Thanksgiving, flutes, autumn leaves, ballet, cats, and old photos.

Launi lives in Orem, Utah, with her husband Devon, their three daughters, and two sons. This is her first juvenile novel.

More about
The Latter-day Daughter Series

After reading Clarissa's story be sure to enjoy the other books in the Latter-day Daughter's Series. They are about girls just like you who lived in other times and places. Read about Anna, who was a special friend to the Prophet Joseph Smith, Laurel who braved the frightening days at Haun's Mill, Maren who discovered a brand new way to be happy—and watch for many more! These stories of adventure, laughter, tears, and fun have been written just for you.